Spiders

Written by Gill Munton

Speed Sounds

Consonants   *Ask children to say the sounds.*

f	l	m	n	r	s	v	z	sh	th	ng
ff	ll		nn		ss	ve	zz			nk
							s			

b	c	d	g	h	j	p	qu	t	w	x	y	ch
bb	k		gg			pp		tt	wh			tch
	ck											

Each box contains one sound but sometimes more than one grapheme.
*Focus graphemes for this story are **circled**.*

Vowels

Ask children to say the sounds in and out of order.

a	e	i	o	u
at	hen	in	on	up

ay	ee	igh	ow	oo
day	see	high	blow	zoo

Story Green Words

Ask children to read the words first in Fred Talk and then say the word.

chest   silk   web   plant   crack   insect

trap   stuck   kept   sac   when   hatch

Ask children to say the syllables and then read the whole word.

ab|do|men

Ask children to read the root first and then the whole word with the suffix.

spin → spins   egg → eggs

Vocabulary Check

Discuss the meaning (as used in the non-fiction text) after the children have read the word.

	definition
abdomen	the part of the body where the stomach is
silk	a very fine, strong thread
sac	a thin pouch for holding eggs
hatch	when a baby creature comes out of its egg

Red Words

the	be	are
to	or*	look*
out*	spider*	spiderlings*
they	he	water

* Red Word in this book only

Let's look at spiders!

A spider has:

- 8 legs
- a chest
- an abdomen.

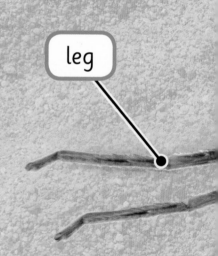

leg

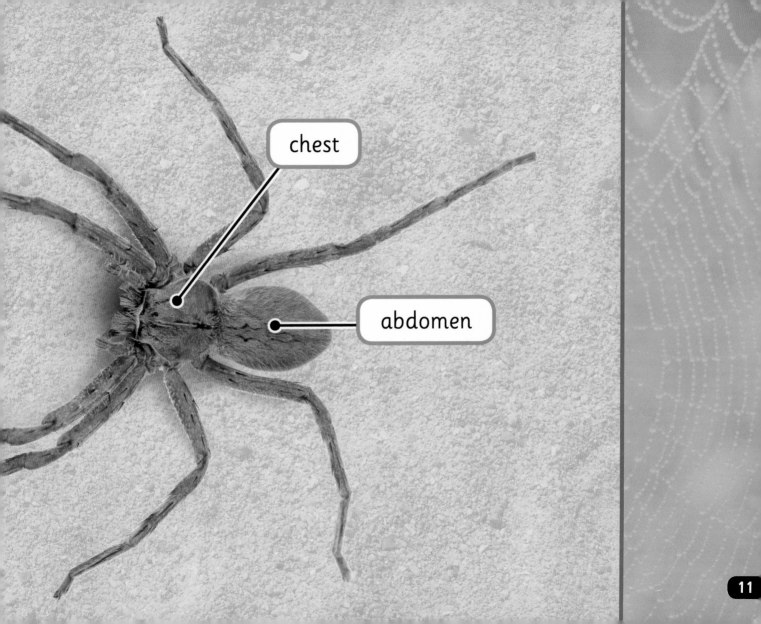

chest

abdomen

A spider spins a silk web.

It can be on a plant or in a crack.

13

The web is an insect trap.

Insects get stuck in it and then the spider can catch them.

Up to 250 spider eggs are kept in an egg sac.

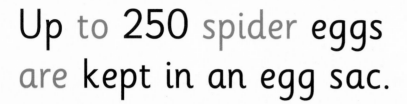

When the eggs hatch, spiderlings run out.

Questions to talk about

Ask children to TTYP for each question using 'Fastest finger' (FF) or 'Have a think' (HaT).

p.10 (FF) How many legs does a spider have?

p.12 (FF) What does a spider spin?

p.13 (FF) Where can you find a spider web?

pp.14–15 (HaT) Why is a spider web useful?

p.16 (FF) Where are spider eggs kept?

Speedy Green Words

Ask children to practise reading the words across the rows, down the columns and in and out of order clearly and quickly.

let's	has	legs
an	can	get
and	then	catch
them	up	run

18